PERSEVERANCE
IN A STRANGE LAND

The Voices of the Youth During the COVID-19 Pandemic

By

DR. STEPHEN L. BOND

Illustration By Anthony Mercer

ARRIE PUBLISHING COMPANY, LLC
PAPERBACK
Cary | New York City | Atlanta | Miami

ARRIE PUBLISHING COMPANY

In loving memory of my twin sister Stephany G. Bond, and two of my co-workers' family members, Gregory Hodge and Oreen Baker, both died of COVID-19 in 2020.
May they Rest in Peace.

TABLE OF CONTENTS

"Every generation leaves behind a legacy. What that legacy will be is determined by the people of that generation. What legacy do you want to leave behind?"

— **John Lewis**

FOREWORD

I have traveled the world for the Harlem Globetrotters and impacted millions of lives. Among those were the lives of youth across this great world, but nothing has been more satisfying than becoming a high school teacher and basketball coach. I have developed such an appreciation of teachers and coaches all over. The impact I have on kids whether it's been with the globetrotters or whether it's at Wilson Preparatory Academy, in Wilson North Carolina, is something I take a lot of pride in and will never take for granted. To be able to help a young man or young woman reach their full potential is a feeling like no other, and the fact that I'm hands-on with them makes it even that more special. To work alongside my friend and brother Stephen Bond and the work that we do with these kids has nothing to do with us. We give all glory to God! This pandemic has been something that has turned a lot of our youths' lives upside down. It's been tough and very discouraging for our young people, and to see a book like this that is written by the youth, is a way to turn all these negatives into positives. I would recommend this book to anybody because it gives people a look inside of what's going on in young people's lives. This book is a light in this time of darkness. I'm proud to say that I love what my brother Stephen Bond has done with this. I've learned in all things that we do and no matter what we go through in life—whether it is negative or positive—we must give God the glory. And, I honestly feel that this is what *Perseverance in a Strange Land* does.

Anthony Atkinson, BS
Teacher/Head Varsity Boys Basketball Coach
Wilson Preparatory Academy

PREFACE

When I received the news that schools would be closed due to the COVID-19 virus in March 2020, I asked my students to keep a journal on how they would feel in the upcoming weeks. While I read their responses, I could feel the pain, sorrow, and frustration in their words. Their responses deeply touched my heart, and I was in awe of their feelings. They told a poignant story, but one filled with hope and optimism. It was at this time that I felt that their work needed to spread not only in Wilson County, North Carolina but all over our country.

What you are about to read is a collection of journals that my students put their whole heart and soul into writing. I have frequently told my students to voice what's on their minds and to also express themselves without hesitation. These students did a tremendous job of doing this, and I am extremely proud of them. They are the future leaders of this world, and they will always be connected with the history of this pandemic. I believe that even years from now, people will read their work as a primary source of information.

While the country was dealing with the pandemic, we also had to deal with another recurring theme in our society and that is racism. The murder of George Floyd sparked an already smoldering fire of racism in this country that had not been rectified. At the end of the book, several of my high school students gave their unadulterated views on the issue of race in America and about the murder of George Floyd. Their bold and passionate replies to these topics could not be ignored.

So as you flip through the pages of this book, please know that it is the concerned voice of the youth. They must be heard so that we can progress as a society. These articulate young men and women who are the authors of this book are the future, and a promising future it is for them!

Dr. Stephen L. Bond
Social Studies Teacher
Wilson Preparatory Academy

CHAPTER 1

The Voices of the Youth in the Midst of a Crisis

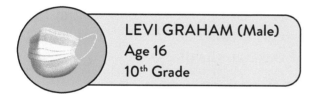

LEVI GRAHAM (Male)
Age 16
10th Grade

March 23–March 25, 2020

Day 1

So, coronavirus kicked me out of school for two weeks. Cool, but I wish it wasn't as dangerous as it is, although I believe that it's been overdramatized for profit and news. People are still doing normal things, for the most part, and no one's gone (sic) rioting for supplies. In my opinion, we don't need to be scared of this. I do believe that it is good to be safe, though. If we can prevent spread (sic) an infection, then let's do that.

Day 2

I wish we could have a normal class today and have some organized structure, but due to Coronavirus2020, we can't do that. I understand that it has no real treatment for it right now and the COVID virus can get dangerous. We see it in

1

Italy. But the toilet paper situation, I do not understand this. We need non-perishable food if there is a real ¨Apocalypse¨ not $200 worth of paper. Be safe, keep calm, play GTA.

Day 3

(Well I've been in here 8 days, but it's officially day 3 of school out.) I feel very socially secluded. I feel even a run to Walmart for some Mike and Ike® would build my spirit. Now, the main reason I am quarantined is that my mom has training in Las Vegas soon that she can't be sick for and waste 7 months of time and wait. I also see my friends around the world online while I'm stuck reading Quadratics. But, now I can say, I've almost lived through the plague of 2020.

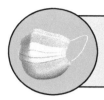

NICHOLAS HYMAN (Male)
Age 18
12th Grade

March 23–April 4, 2020

Week 1

Every day in this quarantine, the atmosphere of the United States changes. It's like this whole pandemic thing doesn't seem real. I know that this pandemic is real, but sitting in the house all the time, thinking that there is a disease out there that people are dying from is so surreal. It really feels like it's a dream that is hard to wake up from.

I also wish that we would've been more prepared for something like this. From the announcement of the virus, it didn't seem as if it was going to be serious. It felt like, we didn't have anything to worry about. I don't understand why something like this had to happen. And, I also don't understand how it happened so fast either. It seemed just like (sic) last week I was at track practice and everything was okay. Now that my school year is over and my senior high school track season is over, I know that I can't let this get me down and affect me in a bad way. I just have to keep pushing and make up for the track season in college. With my senior year over with, I'm really looking forward to my freshman year of college. Hopefully, that won't be affected, and I can be a regular student again.

Week 2

Currently, the coronavirus is progressing. More people are getting sick from it, and we're encouraged to be inside and not go outside if we don't need to. For me, whenever I have to go to the store or go to work, I always take the long way because most of the day, I'm inside doing homework. Also, my sleep schedule is so messed up to the point where I'm awake more than I'm sleeping, and I don't like that one bit.

I think they should just go ahead and pass the people who did their work and have all their credits. For the students who didn't finish, they should get a chance to get all the work they need to do to graduate or move on to the next grade. And being an athlete, I'm missing all the days I could be in the gym, and I have to work out at home which, in some instances, is hard because of distractions and other things. I'm just ready to get this over with, so I can go back to being a regular person.Quarantine doesn't feel good at all. I don't even like being in the house for long periods of time when there isn't (sic) something like this going on. But, I know that there will be an end to this. I just don't know when but hopefully soon.

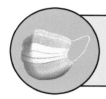

KAILAN WOODARD (Female)
Age 17
11th Grade

March 23–March 27, 2020

What's happening in the world right now feels unreal. It's crazy to think that what's happening now could be in history books in years to come. This is day 5 of not having school, and it feels like an official lockdown. I have so many mixed feelings. I would like to see my friends, but then again, there is that fear of being in contact with someone who might have the virus. I am slowly realizing the things I take for granted, like going shopping or simply eating out with family and friends. These are luxuries that I don't know when they'll return. I do like having the feeling of safety in my home with my family. I can't wait to see how all of this will end up.

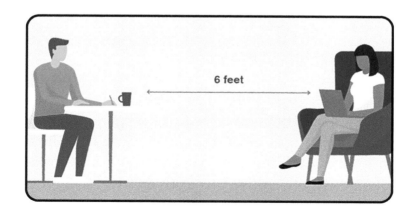

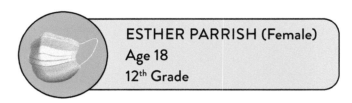

ESTHER PARRISH (Female)
Age 18
12th Grade

March 16–March 20, 2020

JOURNAL

Monday, March 16, 2020

The first day of quarantine from the virus, no school, and I am doing good. I miss the fifth graders that I help every day in math. They are some of the sweetest fifth graders. When I help them and see they finally get *it*, I feel so happy. Today I didn't practice social distancing though. I had to go to Greenville and pick up my bridesmaid dress for my cousin's wedding. His fiancée asked me to be a bridesmaid on Christmas Eve. Today financial aid awards from ECU came out. When I read the emails, I was shocked. I knew my EFC (Expected Family Contribution) wasn't great. But, because of the amount I got, I was surprised. When I got home, I started crying to my dad.

Tuesday, March 17, 2020

Tuesday, again, I and my dad (sic) still didn't practice social distancing. It got him in trouble. My aunt fussed him out which was pretty funny. My aunt wanted us to stay inside because me and him both need to stay in. He has health issues, and he is elderly. He had heart surgery way before I was born which he needs to focus on because I don't want him getting sick with the virus. Today I and my father (sic) went to the store and literally everything was off the shelf. People were taking stuff off the shelf as stuff was being put on the shelf. I just wanted some Goldfish®. Goldfish® were nowhere to be found. Bread was gone. There were no eggs anywhere. We had to end up calling my aunt to find some things for us.

Wednesday, March 18, 2020

Today I was supposed to hang out with my roomie from ECU (GO PIRATES!). She lives in Raleigh, which is like 45 minutes from my house. We were supposed to hang out because our Pirates aboard day @ecu got canceled due to how many people were attending. My aunt made us wait. We are fine with that. We still have Snapchat and Instagram to talk through. It was kind of boring though today. I finished some work for my online accounting and journalism classes. The work was fairly easy. I keep seeing on a parent page, for our school, how parents claim the work our teachers give us has taken their kids 13+ hours to complete daily. I don't think it should take us that long, but maybe, it does for them. Who knows. Quarantine day 3 is good but boring.

Thursday, March 19, 2020

Quarantine day 4 is one of the best days yet. I played Fortnite again with my best friend (online) from Massachusetts. He was the very first friend I ever made on my PS4, and I am glad we are still friends. We won no games, but the thought of us playing Fortnite together was amazing. I love playing the game with him. We only really play together anymore. My financial aid physical letter for college came in today, and I cried again. I've always dreamed of going to college and studying construction management. I only need less than $10k for school (6k or less because of scholarships). This is great. I will be able to attend my school of dreams. Today, I broke social distancing, again, by going out to Cookout restaurant. Best restaurant around in my opinion. All restaurants are going to be drive-thru only. Cookout was wrapped around after I left. Chick-fil-A was wrapped around as well. Sit-down restaurants that had previously been made close dine-in put tables outside. Today, they were made to bring them in.

Friday, March 20, 2020

Today, our President Trump made history by declaring all public schools will be canceled this year. This is very important for teachers and us as students. Teachers and students now have no testing anxiety, but now, both have anxiety for the fact that they have to be prepared for the next grade. Seniors are still shaken at the fact that graduation and prom might be canceled. But for me, I am still going. I'm still doing my daily assignments as I am determined to graduate. I have great plans for me. I have to go to ECU in the fall. It has always been my dream to go there. I will definitely go.

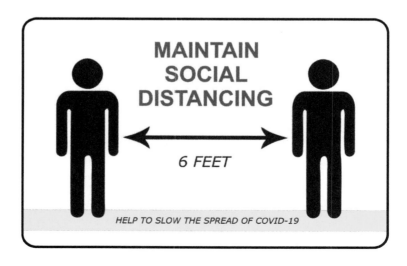

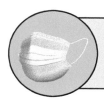

JOSE BUSTOS (Male)
Age 17
11th Grade

March 18, 2020

Civics and Economics Mr. Bond—It's March 18, 2020, and as of today, there are only 2 confirmed cases in Wilson, North Carolina. During this time of quarantine, I've been doing my schoolwork and staying at home but only going out of my house when necessary. In the midst of this pandemic, most people are still going out and risking not only their health but the health of others around them. I am guilty of this because I went to a concert in Raleigh last week when the coronavirus was at its peak in Wake County. Last week before school ended, I went to the doctor because I felt really sick, and I wanted to be sure it wasn't anything serious, but it was just laryngitis. My thoughts on this virus are that no one is safe from it. It won't just kill older people with weaker immune systems. In my opinion, it's selfish of you if you are still traveling for spring break and exposing yourself to the virus because it could hurt your grandparents, parents, or any other family members with weak immune systems. I fear that the whole country could go on quarantine and no one would be able to leave their house.

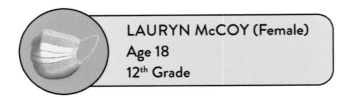

LAURYN McCOY (Female)
Age 18
12th Grade

March 23, 2020

How has the Covid-19 affected me? Well first, I probably won't experience my first prom, and my graduation won't (sic) be the same. There will be no senior trips. The rest of my senior year has been ruined.

I feel like 12 years of going through school is going to waste. How has it affected my social and home life? First off, my mom is on the frontline during this time. She's a respiratory therapist, and I can't remember the last time I hugged my mom or had a full conversation with her. I've seen her cry and breakdown because of this. Because she's worried, she's going to bring it home to me. She has to wear protection, head to toe, every time she comes (sic) into work. I can't be around her anymore.

Socially, I can't go on any dates and see my friends. I won't be able to have a spring break. I miss going inside restaurants and going into my favorite stores. I miss feeling like a normal teenage girl. I'm barely working now and making money to pay bills. It's not normal. It's very weird, and it doesn't seem to feel real. I feel like my life has been put on pause. I wish people would take this more seriously and stay home. You're risking your life and others and possibly making it to the point where we won't have a summer. I'm just ready for our lives to press play.

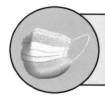

PAYTON TONY WINSTEAD (Male)
Age 18
12th Grade

March 23–March 29, 2020

Journal on Coronavirus and its impact. This virus has made me see a different side of people, including myself. Now I see how much we take for granted now that it's taken away from us, like eating in restaurants, school, going to stores, and even hanging out with our friends. Another scary thing is that if I were to get this virus, it would end my father's life. After he had his heart transplant, his immune system is at its weakest point, so if the virus latched onto him, it would be awful. Just knowing that I could kill my own dad if I contract this virus is making me question my every move that a few months ago was just human nature to me.

The one thing I miss more than being able to go to the store and out to eat is my friends and teachers at school. It's funny how we aren't really the type of kids to look forward to getting up and going to school, but as soon as we are forced to stay away from it, our emotions change. Being a senior in high school and not being able to go to the prom with my high school sweetheart is depressing. Not being able to walk the stage for graduation and let our parents shed the tears of happiness, seeing their child progress into the real world, hurts as well. Last but not least, not being able to have a senior trip with friends you may never even see again just doesn't seem real to me.

It's almost weird how fast this virus came about. I never thought that it would bring the world to these circumstances. I would like to thank all my friends and teachers at Wilson Prep for turning me into the person I am today. If it wasn't for you guys, I'm not (sic) sure where I would be today. Hopefully, I'll be able to see you all again soon.

Sincerely,
Payton

BRAEVEON COOPER (Male)
Age 18
12th Grade

March 23–April 3, 2020

March 23, 2020

I must say that it is getting pretty boring sitting in this house all day. All there is (as of now) is my mom working from home on Tuesdays and Thursdays and my cat, Chloe. Other days it's just me and Chloe. Some days my dad will (sic) come home from his travels, and I would sometimes go out to get food.

I still can't believe it though. The Senior class of 2020 is RUINED by a virus. We had high hopes of graduating and going to prom. People said that 2020 was going to be a movie. Now that Movie seems (sic) is called "Home Alone."

April 3, 2020

It's another week, and yet, I'm still not scared, nor infected (sic) of this virus. But this is for certain: my grandpa needs to visit a doctor IMMEDIATELY.

He's complaining about flu-like symptoms, yet he won't visit a doctor no (sic) matter how much my mom pressures and begs him to. And the fact that my grandpa (and probably others in the house) might be one of the 1 million people with coronavirus concerns me.

But, on another topic, while I'm remaining hopeful, I kind of miss school, yet I don't. I don't miss it because I love being able to wake up later and then watching (sic) TV while I do my work, but I miss school because I just don't (sic) like online classes that well.

Anyways, that's pretty much it for this week. Let's see what happens next.

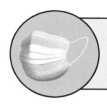

BRANDON BARNES (Male)
Age 18
12th Grade

March 17–April 8, 2020

March 17, 2020

March 16th was the official start of remote learning and staying indoors because of the Coronavirus. My brief understanding of the coronavirus is that it's a contagious virus that can enter a person's system without symptoms. The virus can be passed on through touching, interacting with other individuals, and any other social gestures. This virus is 10 times more lethal than the flu, according to White House officials.

The Coronavirus is shaking the economic, social, medical, and scientific foundations that people live and rely on in the United States and internationally. Schools have been closed due to this. Some kids went to school because it was a way out of their abusive households, a way of making friends, and potentially eating their only meal of the day at school. Everyone is affected by this pandemic and unity is one of the many concepts that is being expressed among people around the world.

March 20, 2020

It's been 4 days since the start of staying indoors due to the Coronavirus. This experience wasn't really a big deal for me since I liked to stay indoors anyway. But, I've been able to maintain my composure and my family has as well. Luckily, video games, TV shows, music, and family have been enough for me to pass the time.

March 25, 2020

Today marks a very important event during the Coronavirus pandemic. Governor Roy Cooper has announced that schools will remain close through May 15 and grades for physical classes with stop as of March 13. He also announced that starting on March 28 everyone in North Carolina will be ordered to stay at home and only go out for essential things like for groceries, medications, etc.

This has brought me to the realization that I may not have graduation to look forward to and wear my chords for Beta Club, National Honor Society, and for being an Eagle Scout and Junior Marshall. I won't have a senior picnic and remember the people that I've known for many years, most of which I have known since the beginning of Wilson Preparatory Academy. I won't be able to say goodbye to the people in school every day of the week. The rest of the school year could possibly be over for me, and I won't be able to experience what other seniors enjoyed in the past.

March 26, 2020

I've been tracking the Coronavirus (COVID-19), ever since the first case has been confirmed in the United States. After the first instance of COVID-19, I became even more concerned when North Carolina's first case was confirmed in Wake County. This deadly disease is going to be the biggest calamity I witnessed in my lifetime.

During this time, family is crucial for people to keep a

sense of sanity. My father is at risk because he is disabled due to a horrific incident, resulting in him having a stroke. Both my sisters are at risk because one has a heart condition that resulted from her going into cardiac arrest when she was 8 years old. My other sister suffers from anxiety and PTSD, which can worsen due to her being in the house and worrying about what has and can happen.

This viral disease is altering the reality of which we, as individuals, are living in. 2020 (sic) was supposed to be the fresh start of many people's lives and now, it may be the end for those same dreamers. The people who lived through this will have a perspective that's precious to modern American history and will be told for generations.

April 3, 2020

Thiswholeexperiencehasbeenhard,butnotoverwhelming. Being in my home gave me a feeling of disconnection from the outside world. Being socially disconnected has been a real struggle and seeing others struggle even more is what makes this experience harder than it seems. But, life has a blunt way of making you realize how precious your life is, and you should never take a day for granted. I hope this pandemic doesn't make things more difficult than they are.

April 8, 2020

Today marks the most important day during the Coronavirus pandemic. I'm a proud recipient of the Golden Leaf Scholarship, which will pay $12,000 every year I'm in college. The scholarship will provide me with a paid job that will help develop my leadership qualities. I'll make up to $8,000 throughout three summers, so I may not have to work in a restaurant or a grocery store. And, I'm scheduled to have an interview done with the Wilson Daily Times about my experience.

However, this huge achievement doesn´t help the fact that my senior year may very well be over, and I won't be able to interact with my fellow classmates. But, things happen for a reason, and I believe that through the struggles I endured throughout my life, this day will be forever embedded in my memory and can be used as motivation through this tragic time. This day will be by far the best day during the Coronavirus pandemic.

My Last Thoughts

The Coronavirus may be known as a disease that kills millions of people, is 10 times more lethal than the flu, and causes people to socially disconnect from others, but it, also, showed how united people around the world can be. This pandemic didn't break the positive mentalities of a lot of people, and in fact, caused those same mentalities to be even more positive. COVID-19 may be the disease that can kill, but it will never kill the spirits and unity that everyone around the world has expressed.

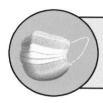

JADEN NORDEN (Male)
Age 16
11th Grade

March 19, 2020

Mr. Bond's Civics—Right now, it has been almost a week since the virus broke out and closed everything and caused people to quarantine themselves. Stores are mostly out of wipes, toilet paper, and paper towels, along with a shortage of canned goods and milk. I stocked up on a bunch of things I like to have, so I would not have to go back into town.

On Tuesday, I got laid off at work because the business was slow, so after this next paycheck, I won't be getting any more money until the sales go back up and they let me work again. I'm going to have to ration my money until then, so I won't be able to spend any of my money for the most part. I have been having to do my school from home, and my church and youth group all got canceled.

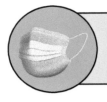

SERA HILL (Female)
Age 15
10th Grade

March 16–March 20, 2020

March 16, 2020

On the first day of being out of school for at least two weeks, it all feels a little surreal. You wouldn't ever imagine that your school would close for two weeks because of a worldwide virus. I think a lot of scholars and parents would agree that the switch to all online work is a little frustrating for both. There are a lot of factors to put into play. Some students do not have internet, food, or parents to stay with them. This is what stresses a lot of parents out, too, because they are worried their kids won't be able to get what they need.

This also makes you wonder how the schools are going to handle this situation as far as grades, end-of-year exams, or even graduation! What if the senior class of 2020 has to graduate virtually? A lot of fun activities that were originally planned will now be canceled for the rest of the school year. It will be very interesting to see how all of this plays out as well as our country and other nations, across the world, handle the pandemic.

March 17, 2020

Today was officially the first day of all online classes at Wilson Preparatory Academy. Understandably, it was a little confusing trying to figure out how to pace out assignments; specifically, when instructors wanted them done. But fortunately, with most of our assignments being online, to begin with, it was easy to adapt. The teachers did very well with the communication process. They made sure that students and parents were very well informed and made sure to describe what you were supposed to be doing in detail. I think that the online classes process should be fine.

March 18, 2020

On Wednesday, my aunt, sister, and I went to Harris Teeter to get a few things. My aunt had us stay in the car for precautionary measures, but the parking lot was insane! To be sure, all the meat was gone, and the cleaning and toilet paper aisles were practically empty. It seems as though everyone was panicking over this virus. Personally, I don't get the toilet paper thing, but hey, that's what the shoppers wanted. I guess people think that the grocery stores are going to shut down? It definitely is a possibility.

I know that all this shopping has definitely affected our stock market. It has caused it to crash from all this panic from the virus. Businesses, restaurants, malls, shopping cen-ters, etc. are all forced to close or serve their customers in a safer way. I guess that means Mr. Jeff Bezos is doing well from the extra wave of online shopping?

March 19, 2020

Today, not much has been going on really. I have become pretty adapted to the whole school thing now, so I'm no longer concerned. I feel as though, as long as we are in contact with our teachers, we should be fine. I hope that we can get the two week period over with and hopefully get back into a real classroom.

Did you know that some schools have already shut down

for the rest of the school year? Schools in Florida, Kansas, and Arizona have already shut down, and California says that they may be next. That makes me wonder if North Carolina would do the same? I hope not. Think of how complicated that would make your transcript or just credits in general.

March 20, 2020

Yay! We actually completed our first week of online schooling! It feels good to get it all done and still get grades in. With that said, there still are a lot of kids who do not have Wi-Fi and do not have anyone to rely on for the internet. Did you know that Spectrum has been so booked trying to help families get free Wi-Fi for 60 days to complete work? It's nice of them to offer it, but there is such a long waiting list that some kids can't get it when they need it.

All we can hope for is that the students who can't get their internet, can find another option or won't (sic) be hurt too badly by it. Hopefully, the virus will finally hurry up and run its course. This way parents and students can get back to their daily lives. I hope you have enjoyed this daily journal!

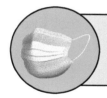

Ms. ALICIA HARRIS (Female)
Age 15
9th Grade

March 17–March 31, 2020

March 17, 2020

My thoughts on this virus are I'm ready for it to go away. Basically, we can't do anything. They don't want us in no (sic) more than groups of 10. We can't eat inside of fast food places. They are canceling some flights. It's just a lot going on. Am I scared? No (sic) not at all. There's nothing to really be scared of because I know if I just stay in the house, I won't (sic) get it. I also serve a God who's covering me through this whole thing, so I have nothing to worry about. I am so ready to get back to school because I like to be in a classroom rather than to have online classes, definitely, when you have more than one. I pray for the ones who do have it in the world, it goes away, and everything can go back to normal.

March 18, 2020

I'm back again and I still have the same feelings. I have heard the news that some schools are now closed for the remainder of the year because of the virus. I pray Wilson prep doesn't close because we need to go back. Also, it'll be good for the seniors, so they can graduate and walk the stage that day. I've also heard that fast food dining areas are closed. I think that is a good idea though, because if they don't want us around more than 10 people, then they do need to close it. After all, there could be 50 people inside. Some schools have online classes for us so that we could still get our education, but I have heard public schools may not. Though, I feel like they need to start online classes because going two weeks without doing work or learning nothing that pertains to school, is horrible. Everyone just needs to stay inside, don't worry, and pray this will be all over soon. I'm praying this will be over sooner than we think.

March 19, 2020

They are now talking about closing the schools until September. This is just ridiculous. I can't believe this is really happening to us. Now they are deciding if I can go to the next grade by me doing all of my assignments. I thought this was going to be over soon, but it seems like it's not. This doesn't mean I'm going to stop praying because prayer changes things.

March 26, 2020

They are now saying the U.S. has more known cases than any other country. To be honest, I'm not even surprised. Sad to say, but I'm not. Right now at least 81,321 people in the United States, are known to have been infected with the Coronavirus. In Florida, there are a total of 2,355 cases. Out of that number 28 have died. In Illinois, there are now 2,538 cases and 26 deaths. It's really a praying time. This is really serious, and I don't think people are realizing that yet.

March 31, 2020

Going on week 3 and my opinion on the virus has not changed one bit. I still feel we just need to stay in the house and listen to what the governor wants us to do, so we can stay safe. How I'm dealing with this is praying and staying in the house. I feel like this is the best thing to do. Yes, I definitely miss school a lot. I miss my friends and my teachers, and I'm ready to go back.

PLEASE WASH YOUR HANDS

ISAIAH PARKER (Male)
Age 17
11th Grade

March 22–March 26, 2020

March 22, 2020

Wow. Imagine not having to wake up early to go to school for once. Imagine how the whole world can change because of one virus. Supposedly, the coronavirus is an easily spread virus between people. But as they say on the news, it can be deadly for elderly people. As for me, I'm not going anywhere until this ends.

March 23, 2020

The one positive about this pandemic to me is that I can stay home and do what I want while managing my work. I do most of my work on Monday so that the rest of the week I can try to enjoy it. However, I do wish I could go to the gym and play basketball. I do miss my family and friends dearly.

March 24, 2020

Today, I woke up thinking I had a free day to do anything I wanted. Well, that was a no. Ever since the state of North Carolina issued no school, I have been getting constant emails about online work and attendance. Basically, it's as if we were still in school. However, I usually do most of my work at the beginning of the week so that I can do what (sic) towards the end of the week.

March 25, 2020

No open gym. No workouts. No basketball training. Sheesh! Only thing I can do is work out at home. The good news is that I can call and text my teammates and check on them. My coach checks on us every day of the week. I miss seeing my coach every day. He is a great person! The number of people dying from the coronavirus is crazy. I hope doctors work together to find a cure instead of working alone, trying to compete on who finds a cure first.

March 26, 2020

Honestly, I don't even know when this pandemic will come to an end. Hopefully, soon but nobody knows. However, this pandemic has given me plenty of time to focus on myself and my future. I get to do a lot of research about our country. I'm learning more about how the government works with laws being passed. I have time to work out as well. I like how I have time to take care of my body because of this pandemic. This is the perfect time to practice eating better. Meanwhile, I really miss seeing some of my teachers and friends. Had no idea how much I would actually miss them. I had so much fun in school and now, it's gone. Hopefully, not for long.

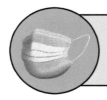

DEVIN REYES (Male)
Age 15
10th Grade

March 23–March 27, 2020

In advance, I want to apologize for how my work has been. This has been my honest view on what (sic) with the past week has been and through it. I've tried to ignore the virus because it scares me and makes my body shake. But overall, my week has been indoors, bored out of my mind, and the same feelings.

Day 1

Monday, March 23, 2020

It's kinda scary how close the virus is near us. I'm not gonna lie here, but I'm glad we're not (sic) at school. But for the most part, I wasn't that fazed by it. We were going to get put anyways (sic). The one thing I hate is that all the work is being assigned, and we have to do them (sic). Kinda sucks, but I guess it makes sense. It's been a lot of fun not being at school though.

Days 2 and 3

Tuesday, March 24, 2020 & Wednesday, March 25, 2020

Nothing has really changed since day one. I've been doing my work for my other classes while paying no mind to the deadly virus outside. None of my family and friends have been affected by this epidemic, which is quite nice. The days seem to be longer and more boring as each hour passes, but it's fine I guess. I wish that the teachers didn't give us a lot of work. Overall, it seems all of the nations, in the world, seem to be taking this virus seriously, except the UK, as many have it there.

Days 4 and 5

Thursday, March 26, 2020, & Friday, March 27, 2020
Things seem to be slowing down when it comes to new information on the virus. President Trump has been active in giving information to the people on what's to come. Italy, along with the UK, is probably the second nation having a major crisis on the virus. For the most part, it seems the world leaders are taking action. I'm happy that everyone (or mostly everyone) is taking this seriously. But overall, living in history really sucks now.

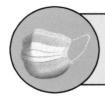

CHARKERA HINNANT (Female)
Age 18
12th Grade

March 24, 2020

With only being one week and a half into the coronavirus pandemic, to me, it's been very interesting to research and discover what has been happening in just a few little days. I've been watching the news and reading a whole bunch of articles. It surprised me a little because I never usually look at the news or read news articles, but I'm just so interested in knowing what's going on in N.C. and in our world right now. Now with all of the salons, barbershops, and so many more places shutting down, it's starting to look like a ghost town in Wilson, and I've never, in my 18 years of living, ever seen my city so empty.

I'm also finding out that I won't be going back to school until May 15th. I was pretty sad. The reason why I'm sad about that is I will definitely miss my friends and some of my favorite teachers. Also, just being stuck in the house is no fun at all, and yes, I do be in contact with my friends, but it's not (sic) the same being in their presence and having fun with them. I've never been in quarantine before, so having this pandemic going on is a very different change and a very different environment than I've been trying to adjust to, and hopefully, everything will go back to normal before the date they gave us for our freedom to come back to school.

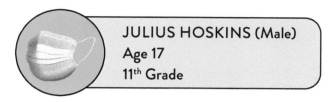

JULIUS HOSKINS (Male)
Age 17
11th Grade

March 22–March 28, 2020

During this first couple of days being out of school because the coronavirus has been a lifestyle changer and has alternated the way I and my family function (sic). My family and I are now more cautious than ever about germs and sanitation. During this time, the virus has made it difficult to travel and move how I want—for example the many stores and facilities that have closed.

I'm a sports fan and because of this epidemic, it has restricted me from watching all the sports I love. I miss being able to hang out with my friends and also being able to play sports during the spring. I have played baseball for the last two years, and I'm already missing it! All school events, such as the prom and class trips, will be most likely canceled, and I won't be able to experience them.

I'm mostly not afraid of the coronavirus because I believe that God is going to get us through it. I pray that this struggle does not continue throughout the year and that it will be over soon.

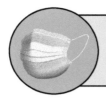

ALBERTO HERRERA STEPHEN (Male)
Age 16
11th Grade

March 18, 2020
Bond Civics and Economics . . . First Week of COVID-19 Pandemic

My name is Alberto Herrera, and I am a sixteen-year-old young man in Wilson, North Carolina. This is currently the first week of the United States being affected by the pandemic known as COVID-19. Cities are on lockdown, schools all across the country are closed, grocery stores are going empty, and billions of people, across the entire world, are being affected in one way or another. Today, I am writing to potentially share a primary source to people of the future. This pandemic will go down in history books, and maybe this small journal can give some insight into the virus that will never be forgotten.

Countless people are being affected. It has gotten to the point where many companies are shutting down to prevent the spread of the virus. Movie theaters, shopping malls, restaurants, gyms, and retail stores are some of the many places that are all closed in an attempt to prevent this virus from spreading. With all these places closed, one could ask: what about all of the people that pay their bills by working at these places? To tell the truth, I don't know the exact answer, but I do know that the virus is definitely impacting our economy.

Even though this virus isn't the deadliest, it affects older-aged people and even those with weaker immune systems. As for me, I have been home for the past five days, and I have only left the house twice. Since my dad is older and diabetic, my family is doing everything we can to be safe.

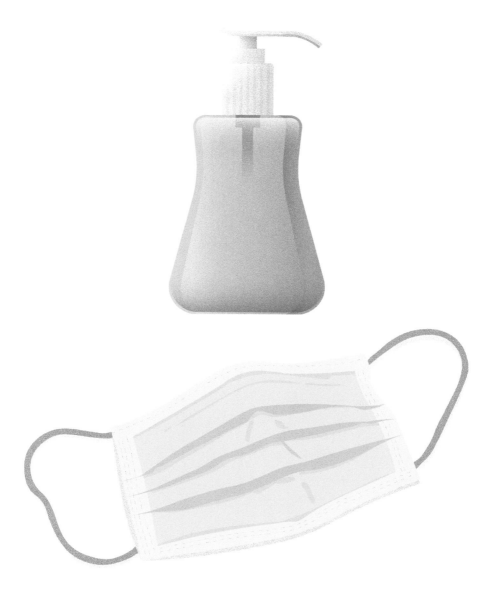

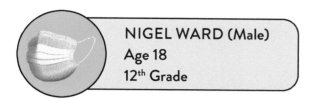

NIGEL WARD (Male)
Age 18
12th Grade

March 15–March 21, 2020

The coronavirus has really taken over the earth, and I've never experienced anything like this before. This is a huge pandemic that has made the world completely stop. All schools are closing down, people are being asked to stay inside, and people with the virus are being quarantined. Last but not least, the fear of wondering if you're going to be next (sic). These past few days haven't really been that bad for me, but I feel like the virus is going to get worse and spread more as the days go by. I'm mainly scared for the elderly and people with weak immune systems because they are saying that's who the virus mainly affects. It's been pretty boring, too, with this virus around, not being able to leave the house without any worries. It's like everything I see now is related to the virus in some way whether it's watching TV or just surfing the internet. Lastly, I want to say that I hope this virus passes over and we can all go back to our normal lives because I don't want to see any of my loved ones die because of this pandemic.

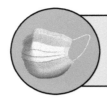

NASIAR BLACKSTON (Male)
Age 17
11th Grade

March 18, 2000

As we go through this phase of the coronavirus, my feelings about this are mixed. I feel confused, upset, sad, and stressed. The confusion I have is why is it hitting us now. Why is this affecting my life? I'm upset and sad because my life is built around basketball. I have not been to the gym to work on my skill set since last week. I fear I may get complacent and end up being a nobody for basketball again. I fear this coronavirus will harm the people I love and care about. I don't really have a lot of feelings through this cause (sic) every day I pray. I know God will show us the way and cure us of all evil that stands in our way.

JACOB HUFFMAN (Male)
Age 15
10th Grade

Week 3 - March 29, 2020 - April 3, 2020

Sadly, Dr. Bond, I feel like the situation has only gotten worse, and it is having a drastic effect on me. I have been stressing out to the point that I feel like I'm having panic attacks, and I don't know how to control it. I have been praying that everything sorts itself out. And, my aunt has fallen ill, and doctors have said she won't live past six months. And, I still don't know if I have it in me to see another relative in a casket. Plus, trying to keep up with biology and math is a continuous struggle because my ability to learn is handicapped with not having the face to face teaching, along with how difficult they have made math already. But despite everything, I still try my hardest every day to do good and look on the bright side, but it feels like my sparks are fading every day.

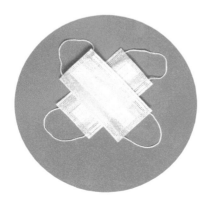

CHAPTER 2

The Youths' Views Concerning the Murder of George Floyd

The Murder of George Floyd

The date May 25, 2020, brought a devastating blow to an already fractured country. On that day, George Floyd, a 46-year-old black American man, was killed by a Minneapolis, Minnesota police officer, during an arrest for allegedly using a counterfeit bill at a convenience store. The police officer who killed him was Derek Chauvin, a white man who had 18 complaints on his official record, two of which ended in discipline, including official letters of reprimand. He had been involved in police shootings, one of which was fatal.

A bystander videoed the incident that took place which recorded Chauvin kneeling on George Floyd's neck for approximately eight minutes. During the graphic video, Mr. Floyd is repeatedly telling Chauvin that he cannot breathe. Chauvin ignores Mr. Floyd and bystanders pleas to remove his knee. Three other Minneapolis, Minnesota police officers were at the scene, Officers J. Alexander Kueng and Thomas Land were further restraining George Floyd while Officer Tou Thao was preventing bystanders from interfering.

Former Officer Derek Chauvin didn't remove his knee off

Mr. Floyd's neck until paramedics told him to do so. George Floyd eventually died at the scene.

Videos made by the bystanders and security camera soon turned public. Throughout the United States and eventually the world, people witnessed George Floyd being killed by a police officer who was supposed to serve and protect, not murder an individual without justice cause. Once the autopsy report by Hennepin County medical examiner and an independent medical autopsy commissioned by Mr. Floyd's family came back, revealing the cause of Mr. Floyd's death—mechanical asphyxia—and the death was listed as a homicide, Officer Derek Chauvin was fired from the police department and charged with third-degree murder and second-degree manslaughter. Later, second-degree murder was added to his list of chargers. His fellow officers were fired and then charged with aiding and abetting second-degree murder.

The death of George Floyd triggered protests against police brutality, police racism, and lack of accountability. Unrested followed. The protesting started locally in Minneapolis-Saint Paul, but soon spread nationwide and in over 60 countries, supporting the Black Lives Matter Movement.

As a bonus, several students wrote their feelings about the murder of George Floyd and their views on how race impacts the United States.

NASIAR BLACKSTON
Rising Senior
Age 17
African American Male

To me, the color of someone's skin can mean several things. Sadly, people are being labeled by the color of their skin every day. And, it bothers me because it happens every day! It's not right to be judged, but it seems like that's how life is.

I feel, however, that no one should be judged by the color of their skin. Every day it seems black people are being stereotyped as gangsters or thugs. I, myself, have been labeled multiple times because I'm black, and this was even before I had started to play basketball. I've had police officers come to me and grab me as if I did something wrong. I've even been put in handcuffs because supposedly I matched a description of a criminal! My skin color is not a weapon. It is a part of who I am!

I feel the death of George Floyd was something that shouldn't have been done. I feel that it started a conflict that might never finish. People are still protesting as we speak about his death. His death has shown the true colors of people in many ways! It has shown that people are fighting against racism in this country, but many racists have shown they are willing to defend the racist past of this country.

MALIK BRYANT
Rising Senior
Age 17
Biracial Male

The color of an individual's skin has a major impact on society. Many people assume that because of the color of their skin, they're either privileged or a threat to our community. Different races shouldn't have to be seen as a threat due to their color. They should be treated the same as any other race and shouldn't have to fear going out in public. This impacts our society because many races of people are stereotyped. And it's stereotypes that help create racism in our country.

Being a biracial young man, (being mixed with African American and White) I feel that the George Floyd murder by police officers was horrible! Floyd, being a black man, was labeled as a target by them due to race. George Floyd was an innocent man and father who screamed several times he couldn't breathe, and the police officer still kneeled on his back! If that was a white man instead of a black man, the officers would've definitely treated him differently! There have been white people who have been accused of more violent things than Floyd was accused of and weren't treated as harshly. We must do better as a nation!

CAMERON BRYANT
Rising Junior
Age 16
Biracial Male

In our society, race and color have a major impact on this country. I am biracial (from my parents), and I don't think of myself any different from anybody else. When it comes to color, I look at every person as the same. Being a biracial child, thankfully, I was never treated differently from either side of my family. Others on the outside may have looked at us differently, but it doesn't matter to me.

I appreciate and embrace being biracial. I am proud of it and the cultures involved with both. That's to me what makes the beauty of the world. If everyone was the same and had the same culture and ideas, the world would just be plain.

I am so upset about the fact that George Floyd was killed on the street and had his video all over social media! How can people say that nothing was wrong with what happened? He was murdered by police and everyone knows it! Things have to change in our country. We need a better support system from our government. We should never be scared to go out as Black people and think we might be killed! I want things to change for the future and for the kids growing up that they can have peace.

NICHOLAS HYMAN
Graduated from Wilson Preparatory Academy, May 2020
Age 18
African American Male
Attending NC Central University, August 2020

P ersonally, I don't think my skin color and race should have an impact on me in society; however, I know it does. I never had a second thought about it. I never second-guessed that fact. It's sad that we live in a country where the color of your skin can either paint you as a threat or paint you as an unharmful person. In fact, it impacts me being in society so much, to the point, where I love being black, but I hate being black in America. I'd love to be black in another country and not have to worry that if I got stopped by a police officer, I might not make it back home just because "It looked like I had a gun," and I didn't or "The officer feared for his life," and I clearly posed no threat since the only man in this situation with a *Deadly Weapon* is the police officer. So, this begs the question of "Who actually fears for their life in this situation?"

With me being a black man, I feel as though people are synonymous and race doesn't belong here. And, we need to leave the color of my skin out of it. The ongoing racism in this country is sickening. People preach peace and unity, but we all know that the majority don't stand with that idea. They'd rather see chaos and racial bedlam that unity will almost never work. The color of my skin isn't liked by millions of people in this country, and I just don't see why—like I really can't fathom why. It impacts me being in society by making me not want to be in society honestly. I know I'll get funny

looks because of my hair, because of my darker black skin, because of my African features, because of everything. It impacts where I can and can't go even in America today. I know that I can't go to certain places down South because I know what could happen to me. I also know that my skin color impacts what I can buy, where I can buy it, and how I can buy it. Sadly, it also impacts my credibility as well. I just think black people aren't welcome here, and people are making it blatantly obvious. Sadly, many black people don't realize it.

My thoughts on the George Floyd murder are that it's just like how we were killed in the 1800s and 1900s, to be honest. History is repeating itself, but now instead of taking pictures of, for example, a lynching after it happened, we can record it and share it with the whole world. I don't see anything happening, like this, where the police deliberately kill one group of people in any other country. It's genocide, and we're being hunted. I also think that this problem is still going to continue to occur to be quite frank. Because if we're being honest, the police are doing their job. The police were created from runaway patrolmen whose assignment was to catch runaway slaves. But now, we're not slaves anymore, but if they catch you, (which is a traffic stop) they can do whatever they want with you because ninety-nine percent of the time they know that they can kill you and get away with it. I think that the murder was one part of a big plan that's in place by the government, and they won't tell us what happens next. They'll do everything behind the scenes that they don't want us to see, while basically, the whole country is fighting against each other like a second Civil War. And then while each side is down and vulnerable, they'll unveil what they did and are planning to do.

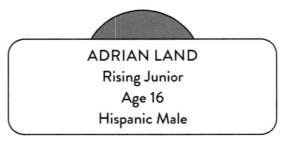

ADRIAN LAND
Rising Junior
Age 16
Hispanic Male

When people understand that the color of one's skin is just that . . . the color of their skin, it shouldn't make you superior or inferior to another person in any way; it is simply the melanin pigment in your skin! When people understand that we are all one race, the human race, people will be able to judge people not by the color of their skin but by the content of their character. Change doesn't happen overnight, but it starts here with us. If we don't make the change, who will.

The color of one's skin in American society can have many meaningless effects on a person. Racial profiling, police brutality, and hate crimes are real. They are taking place all over America, and it is unacceptable. We cannot truly be a free nation until all people within it are truly free. Feeling unsafe around an officer is not how it should be; you should feel protected and not have to wonder if your life could come to an end at the hands of a police officer.

KEVIN FARMER
Rising Senior
Age 17
African American Male

I t is sad but true—people do judge you in America by your skin color. Me being a black male, I understand the anger and pain I feel when I'm followed around in stores, or people assume I'm not smart because of my skin color. I hope for the day when this racism ends in this country.

My view is that I'm very angry that Greg Floyd was murdered by a police officer. He is seen on camera begging for his life saying, "I can't breathe." Still, his begging was not enough, and he had no right to pass away at all! We must be peaceful in our protests though. I always say you can't fight fire with fire, meaning we can't just have these brutal protestors expecting others to listen. By us destroying property and vandalizing towards others will just make it worse. Doing protests with peace to all is what I prefer because all lives matter in my view.

Dr. Stephen L. Bond

DEVYN BULLOCK
Rising Senior
Age 18
African American Male

George Floyd was an African American male who was killed with excessive force while he was unarmed in police custody. His last words were "I can't breathe," and these three words have led to the riots and protests against social injustice. We've had one's skin color or race affect people in society in numerous ways. Color or race can affect the way you are viewed, which can lead to you not being able to get employment and a variety of things. It can also lead to violence and attack without any apparent reason. Racism has affected our world even before slavery began and still continues today for not just African-Americans but for all minorities in general. This takes place in our society every day and nothing seems to help the situation. It seems like nothing was being done until the incidents, such as George Floyd and others.

It seems our society has finally woken up about the injustice we have seen. This has started change throughout many communities and has brought most of our society together so that change can be done.

JASHAUN TAFT
Rising Senior
Age 17
African American Male

I n today's society, the color of your skin can be the deciding factor of whether or not you get a job. It can also be the cause of dirty looks or expressions while you're doing regular grocery shopping. Our society is composed of millions of people who have to live their lives looking over their shoulders for fear of being wrongfully arrested or killed. We live in a society where knowledge isn't always power, and the color of your skin, unfortunately, is where power stems from in our current times. People of color that are in this country are in a system where not speaking out upholds them in a cycle of oppression. And on the other hand, speaking out brings them (sic) constant physical and verbal abuse that is hard to retaliate against.

George Floyd was one of the most recent murder victims who died because of the blatant racism shown by police in this country currently. The same police, who are supposed to be here to protect and serve, seem to be here to harm and kill us black males. George Floyd seemed to be the eye-opener for the public to stand up and no longer accept the systematic oppression existing within the United States. Some of us make the mistake of being blind to history. The system in which we live is not new. It dates back to slavery times when people of color were stripped from their families and homes to work for a plantation owner. They were taken away to work for someone who bled the same color as them, just of different skin color. Our system now is so similar to then! It is time to strip ourselves of our own blindness because as the philosopher George Santayana so famously said, "Those who cannot remember the past are condemned to repeat it."

JACOB HUFFMAN
Rising Junior
Age 16
White

Personally, I feel that my skin color hasn't had an impact on myself in our society, because I try to surround myself with understanding and rationally minded people. I know, however, many people judge others by skin color, and it's what they do.

As for the murder of George Floyd, I was disgusted and appalled when I found out what happened to him. I have watched the news reports of protests, and I agree that we should all stand up against racial violence and come together as a community. However, I don't believe in the violent behavior caused by his death. I understand the anger, but rioting doesn't make the situation any better. If everyone acts as violent as the ones responsible, then how are we better than them? The only way to stop racial violence is to show people that we are the same, and skin color should not matter. So, I stand against racism with my fellow citizens who say *enough is enough*.

BRAEVEON COOPER
Graduated from Wilson Preparatory Academy, May 2020
Age 18
African American Male
Attending East Carolina University, August 2020

Today in society, my race is still seen as somewhat of a danger to people. It seems like I can't go anywhere, feeling as if a white person or any other race will be the ones to deem me as a suspicious person, and will either end up calling the police or taking matters into their own hands and pulling out a gun on me. Even if a police car is behind me, I get scared as if I will be the next person to get killed by an officer. Black people have been oppressed and discriminated against for so long, and it doesn't seem like racism will be going away anytime soon. So, when I saw the murder of George Floyd, I was angered, but not surprised. To me, I feel the criminal justice system was never built to protect us as a race. The police have committed so many crimes against black people that it isn't even surprising anymore. The police officers are often let go or terminated. Even if the officers were arrested, they probably won't be in jail for that long.

Today I'm just seeing videos on Twitter of innocent black lives being oppressed, and some of which lives were unnecessarily lost. It makes me sick to my stomach.

Not all white people are bad. Not all cops are bad. I see the white people protesting for our cause, and I see the cops who kneel for a cause. There are many good cops out there who are just doing their job. Still, to be extra cautious these days for the black people all around the world and especially in the United States, (which is claimed to be the land of the free) be careful and do your own business out there. And, be kind. However, sometimes that may not even be enough to be flagged as suspicious.

Our lives, as African Americans, matter. They mattered then, they matter now, and we should not feel endangered.

DUNCAN BRACEY
Rising Senior
Age 18
White Male

I n modern discourse, especially among white Americans, there is a false notion that we live in a post-racial society. However, the truth for many Americans is that race plays an integral part in the way they encounter the American experience. Whether it be where you live, where you're educated, how you are treated by law enforcement, employment opportunities, or a vast array of other basic experiences, the way you are treated is deeply predicated upon the color of your skin. This isn't to say that no (sic) white person will ever have a rough go of it, or that no (sic) person of color will have a relatively easy go of it. It is, however, indisputable that evidence has consistently shown that white Americans are less likely to be brutalized by the police, paid more on average, have lower infant and maternal mortality rates, less likely to be arrested for drug crimes committed at the same rate as Black Americans, and a plethora of other statistics showing a societal bias for whites. To say, then, that we have solved the problems of racial inequity in this country is clearly false.

The brutal lynching of George Floyd by police is just a small glimpse into the brutalization people of color experience at the hands of police. The common sentiment is that the police system has failed. However, it may be that the police system is just continuing to do what it was originally designed to do. In practice, modern policing has enforced an unwritten, undemocratically adopted version of our law, one that penalizes being born a person of color. One may feel the need to look back to the early 20th century to examine the original sins of policing, and while this will indeed unearth many issues, to find a treasure trove of issues that affect policing today, one must only look to the beginnings of the so-called "war on drugs," a "war" which continues to this day. Doing this small amount of research will help us understand why we must have a bottom-up overhaul of our law enforcement systems in order to enact real, progressive change.

CAMERON MINGA
Rising Junior
Age 16
African American Male

My race in America impacts me in a positive and in a negative way. Being black in America makes me proud. It makes me proud because all of the hate people sometimes give me makes me work harder every day. Not only for myself but for my community as well. I love being black in America. It just makes me feel so different, and I love being different from everyone else in a crowd. Even though I love being black in America, it also scares me at times. It scares me because my life could be taken at any moment just because someone hates the color of my skin, and that really sickens me. Not too many people would agree with this, but I like all the hardships I face as a black man. The reason being is despite all the hardships, I still can become a successful black man in America, while also taking care of my family and my community. That's when I'll sit back and think *I overcame all of these challenges as a black man and all of my people around me are successful because of my hard work.* That is when I'll just laugh in a racists face and say, "I made it in life. You can't get mad at me from being the best by starting from the bottom."

I was very sad about George Floyd's life being taken. It truly broke my heart. There are so many black men being murdered every day but not all of them get the limelight and attention. Many people just don't want to see black men succeed in this world, I feel. That's why most of the racist people become jealous of successful black men and try to harm them. The reason why racism is still going on today is because of ignorance and a lack of changing perspective. People are so ignorant they don't want to believe what they are thinking or doing is wrong, and then they deny it in public.

What I mean by lack of perspective is racists only look at black people, like they would look at the moon, and stereotype them. They see only one side that the TV and social media convey. But, they don't take time to try and learn about the other side of the moon and the culture and greatness we have. That's my view!

CHAPTER 3

Motivational Quotes from Phenomenal People Who Made a Difference

> **"Ask not what your country can do for you—ask what you can do for your country."**
>
> *— President John F. Kennedy*

John Fitzgerald Kennedy (May 29, 1917 – November 22, 1963), often referred to by his initials JFK or by his nickname Jack, was an American politician who served as the 35th President of the United States from January 1961 until his assassination in November 1963. Kennedy served at the height of the Cold War, and the majority of his work as president concerned relations with the Soviet Union and Cuba.

> **"The time is always right to do what is right."**
>
> — *Dr. Martin Luther King, Jr.*

Martin Luther King, Jr. (January 15, 1929 – April 4, 1968) was an American Christian minister and activist who became the most visible spokesperson and leader in the civil rights movement from 1955 until his assassination in 1968. Martin Luther King, Jr. is best known for advancing civil rights through nonviolence and civil disobedience, inspired by his Christian beliefs and the nonviolent activism of Mahatma Gandhi.

Dr. King led the 1955 Montgomery bus boycott and later became the first president of the Southern Christian Leadership Conference (SCLC). He helped organize the nonviolent 1963 protests in Birmingham, Alabama and helped organize the 1963 March on Washington, where he delivered his famous "I Have a Dream" speech on the steps of the Lincoln Memorial.

"**I am a slow walker, but I never walk backwards.**"

— *Abraham Lincoln*

Abraham Lincoln (February 12, 1809 – April 15, 1865) was an American statesman and lawyer who served as the 16th president of the United States from 1861 to 1865. Lincoln led the nation through its greatest moral, constitutional, and political crisis in the American Civil War. He succeeded in preserving the Union, abolishing slavery, bolstering the federal government, and modernizing the U.S. economy.

> "From what we get, we can make a living. What we give; however, makes a life."
> — *Arthur Ashe*

Arthur Robert Ashe Jr. (July 10, 1943 – February 6, 1993) was an American professional tennis player who won three Grand Slam singles titles.

Ashe was the first black player selected to the United States Davis Cup team and the only black man ever to win the singles title at Wimbledon, the US Open, and the Australian Open. He retired in 1980. He was ranked world No. 1 by Harry Hopman in 1968 and by Lance Tingay of The Daily Telegraph and World Tennis Magazine in 1975. In the ATP computer rankings, he peaked at No. 2 in May 1976.

On June 20, 1993, Ashe was posthumously awarded the Presidential Medal of Freedom by the United States President Bill Clinton.

> **"My parents are my backbone. Still are. They're the only group that will support you if you score zero or you score 40."**
>
> *— Kobe Bryant*

Kobe Bean Bryant (August 23, 1978 – January 26, 2020) was an American professional basketball player. He was a shooting guard with the Los Angeles Lakers in the NBA. He spent his entire basketball career with the L.A. Lakers and is regarded as one of the greatest players of all time. Bryant won five NBA championships and was an 18-time All-Star, a 15-time member of the All-NBA Team, a 12-time member of the All-Defensive Team, the 2008 NBA Most Valuable Player (MVP), and a two-time NBA Finals MVP. He also led the NBA in scoring twice. He was born in Philadelphia and partly raised in Italy. He was recognized as the top high-school basketball player in the U.S. while in high school in Pennsylvania. Bryant is the son of former NBA player Joe Bryant and was drafted by the NBA in 1996 after graduating from Lower Merion High School in

Pennsylvania. He was selected by the Charlotte Hornets with the 13th overall pick, and then traded by the Hornets to the Lakers. He and teammate Shaquille O'Neal led the Lakers to three consecutive NBA championships from 2000 to 2002.

Kobe Bryant and his 13-year-old daughter Gianna, along with seven others, died in a helicopter crash in Calabasas, California in January 2020. The death of Kobe Bryant devastated the entire world. Although he is truly missed, his powerful legacy remains.

"There never will be complete equality until women themselves help to make laws and elect lawmakers."

— *Susan B. Anthony*

Susan B. Anthony (February 15, 1820 – March 13, 1906) was an American social reformer and women's rights activist who played a pivotal role in the Women's Suffrage movement. Born into a Quaker family committed to social equality, she collected anti-slavery petitions at the age of 17. In 1856, she became the New York state agent for the American Anti-Slavery Society.

In 1872, Anthony was arrested for voting in her hometown of Rochester, New York, and convicted in a widely publicized trial. Although she refused to pay the fine, the authorities declined to take further action.

"The future rewards those who press on. I don't have time to feel sorry for myself. I don't have time to complain. I'm going to press on."

— *Barack Obama*

Barack Hussein Obama II (born August 4, 1961) is an American politician and attorney who served as the 44th president of the United States from 2009 to 2017. A member of the Democratic Party, Obama was the first African-American president of the United States. He previously served as a U.S. senator from Illinois from 2005 to 2008 and an Illinois state senator from 1997 to 2004. He was the third African American to be elected to that body since the end of Reconstruction (1877). In 2009, he was awarded the Nobel Peace Prize "for his extraordinary efforts to strengthen international diplomacy and cooperation between peoples."

"That little man in black there, he says women can't have as much rights as men 'cause Christ wasn't a woman! Where did your Christ come from? Where did your Christ come from? From God and a woman! Man had nothing to do with Him."

— *Sojourner Truth*

Sojourner Truth (born Isabella "Belle" Baumfree; c. 1797 – November 26, 1883) An abolitionist and women's rights activist, Truth was born into slavery and escaped with her infant daughter to freedom in 1826. She became best known for her "Ain't I a Woman?" speech on racial inequalities in 1851 at the Ohio Women's Rights Convention.

"I had crossed the line. I was free; but there was no one to welcome me to the land of freedom. I was a stranger in a strange land."

— *Harriet Tubman*

Harriet Tubman (born Araminta Ross, c. March 1822 – March 10, 1913) was an American abolitionist and political activist. Born into slavery, Tubman escaped from slavery in 1849 and became a famous "conductor" of the Underground Railroad. Tubman risked her life to lead hundreds of slaves to freedom using a network of antislavery activists and secret network of safe houses known as the Underground Railroad. During the American Civil War, she served as an armed scout and spy for the Union Army. In her later years, Tubman was an activist in the movement for women's suffrage (the right of women by law to vote in national or local elections).

> "Education is the passport to the future, for tomorrow belongs to those who prepare for it today."
>
> — *Malcolm X*

El-Hajj Malik El-Shabazz (May 19, 1925 – February 21, 1965), born Malcolm Little and better known as Malcolm X, was an African American Muslim minister, prominent leader in the Nation of Islam who articulated concepts of race pride and black nationalism in the early 1960s and human rights activist who was a popular figure during the civil rights movement. After his assassination, the widespread distribution of his life story—*The Autobiography of Malcolm X* (1965)—made him an ideological hero, especially among black youth.

> **"Take all the courses in your curriculum. Do the research. Ask questions. Find someone doing what you are interested in! Be curious!"**
>
> *— Katherine Johnson*

Katherine Johnson (August 26, 1918 – February 24, 2020) made the most of limited educational opportunities for African Americans, graduating from college at age 18. She began working in aeronautics as a "computer" in 1952, and after the formation of NASA, she performed the calculations that sent astronauts into orbit in the early 1960s and to the moon in 1969. One of NASA's human 'computers,' Katherine Johnson performed the complex calculations that enabled humans to successfully achieve space flight. Her story is depicted in the 2016 movie 'Hidden Figures.' Johnson was awarded with the Presidential Medal of Freedom in 2015 by President Barack Obama. She passed away on February 24, 2020, at the age of 101.

> **"You create opportunities by performing, not complaining."**
>
> — *Muriel F. Siebert*

Wall Street legend and pioneer **Muriel Faye "Mickie" Siebert** (September 12, 1928 – August 24, 2013) was known as The First Woman of Finance (despite being preceded in owning a brokerage by Victoria Woodhull) because she was the first woman to own a seat on the New York Stock Exchange and was the first woman to head one of the NYSE's member firms. She joined the 1,365 male members of the exchange on December 28, 1967.

"I want history to remember me . . . not as the first black woman to have made a bid for the presidency of the United States, but as a black woman who lived in the 20th century and who dared to be herself. I want to be remembered as a catalyst for change in America."

— *Shirley Chisholm*

Shirley Chisholm (November 30, 1924 – January 1, 2005) is best known for becoming the first Black congresswoman (1968), representing New York State in the U.S. House of Representatives for seven terms. She went on to run for the 1972 Democratic nomination for the presidency— becoming the first major-party African-American candidate to do so. Throughout her political career, Chisholm fought for education opportunities and social justice. Chisholm left Congress in 1983 to teach. She died in Florida in 2005. Shirley Chisholm became the first African American congresswoman in 1968. Four years later, she became the first major-party black candidate to make a bid for the U.S. presidency.

> "When our thoughts—
> which bring actions—
> are filled with hate
> against anyone,
> Negro or white, we
> are in a living hell.
> That is as real as hell
> will ever be."
>
> — *George Washington Carver*

George Washington Carver (born 1860s – January 5, 1943) was an American agricultural scientist, botanist, teacher, and inventor who promoted alternative crops to cotton and methods to prevent soil depletion. His work revolutionized agriculture in the Southern United States. He was the most prominent black scientist of the early 20th century.

When slave holders Moses and Susan Carver moved to Southwest Missouri, they built a small 12' x 12' cabin. Eventually that same cabin was inhabited by an enslaved girl named Mary. She gave birth to George towards the end of the Civil War. George's exact birth day and year are unknown, but it is known that his birth was before Missouri slavery was abolished in January, 1864. As a young child, George's interest in plants was evident earning the nickname of "Plant Doctor" due to his careful tending to a secret garden of cotton depleted. Here he experimented with different types of plants that ultimately formed a burning desire in George for a scientific education tailored to understand and aid him in unlocking botanical secrets.

> **"A winner is someone who recognizes his God-given talents, works his tail off to develop them into skills, and uses these skills to accomplish his goals."**
>
> *— Larry Bird*

Larry Joe Bird (born December 7, 1956) is an American former professional basketball player, coach and executive in the National Basketball Association (NBA). Nicknamed "The Hick from French Lick" and "Larry Legend," Bird is widely regarded as one of the greatest basketball players of all time.

Drafted into the NBA by the Boston Celtics with the sixth overall pick in the 1978 NBA draft, Bird started at small forward and power forward for the Celtics for 13 seasons. Bird was a 12-time NBA All-Star and received the NBA Most Valuable Player Award three consecutive times (1984–1986), making him the only forward in league history to do so. He played his entire professional career for Boston, winning three NBA championships and two NBA Finals MVP awards.

Bird was also a member of the gold-medal-winning 1992 United States men's Olympic basketball team known as "The Dream Team." He was voted to the NBA's 50th Anniversary All-Time Team in 1996, was inducted into the Naismith Memorial Basketball Hall of Fame in 1998, and was inducted into the Hall of Fame again in 2010 as a member of "The Dream Team." He was rated the greatest NBA small forward of all time by Fox Sports in 2016. Bird was also ranked as the greatest Boston Celtics player of all time by MSN Sports in 2018.

"Once I got into space, I was feeling very comfortable in the universe. I felt like I had a right to be anywhere in this universe, that I belonged here as much as any speck of stardust, any comet, and planet."

— *Mae C. Jemison*

Mae Carol Jemison (born October 17, 1956) is the first African American female astronaut. In 1992, she flew into space aboard the Endeavour, becoming the first African American woman in space. She is an American engineer, physician, and former NASA astronaut. She became the first black woman to travel into space when she served as a mission specialist aboard the Space Shuttle Endeavour. Jemison joined NASA's astronaut corps in 1987 and was selected to serve for the STS-47 mission, during which she orbited the Earth for nearly eight days on September 12–20, 1992.

Born in Alabama and raised in Chicago, Jemison graduated from Stanford University with degrees in chemical engineering as well as African and African-American studies. She then earned her medical degree from Cornell University. Jemison was a doctor for the Peace Corps in Liberia and Sierra Leone from 1983 until 1985 and worked as a general practitioner. In pursuit of becoming an astronaut, she applied to NASA.

Jemison left NASA in 1993 and founded a technology research company. She later formed a non-profit educational foundation and through the foundation is the principal of the 100 Year Starship project funded by DARPA. She holds several honorary doctorates and has been inducted into the National Women's Hall of Fame and the International Space Hall of Fame.

> **"We cannot solve our problems with the same thinking we used when we created them."**
>
> — *Albert Einstein*

Albert Einstein (14 March 1879 – 18 April 1955) was a German-born theoretical physicist, who developed the theory of relativity, one of the two pillars of modern physics (alongside quantum mechanics). His work is also known for its influence on the philosophy of science. He is best known to the general public for his mass–energy equivalence formula E=mc2, which has been dubbed "the world's most famous equation." He received the 1921 Nobel Prize in Physics "for his services to theoretical physics, and especially for his discovery of the law of the photoelectric effect," a pivotal step in the development of quantum theory.

"I don't think of myself as a poor deprived ghetto girl who made good. I think of myself as somebody who from an early age knew I was responsible for myself, and I had to make good."

— Oprah Winfrey

Oprah Gail Winfrey (born January 29, 1954) is an American talk show host, television producer, actress, author, and philanthropist. She is best known for her talk show, The Oprah Winfrey Show, broadcast from Chicago, which was the highest-rated television program of its kind in history and ran in national syndication for 25 years from 1986 to 2011. Dubbed the "Queen of All Media," she was the richest

African American of the 20th century and North America's first black multi-billionaire, and she has been ranked the greatest black philanthropist in American history.

Sometimes ranked as the most influential woman in the world, Winfrey was born into poverty in rural Mississippi to a teenage single mother and later raised in inner-city Milwaukee. She has stated that she was molested during her childhood and early teens and became pregnant at 14; her son was born prematurely and died in infancy. Sent to live with the man she calls her father, Vernon Winfrey, a barber in Tennessee, Winfrey landed a job in radio while still in high school. By 19, she was a co-anchor for the local evening news. Winfrey's often emotional, extemporaneous delivery eventually led to her transfer to the daytime talk show arena, and after boosting a third-rated local Chicago talk show to first place, she launched her own production company and became internationally syndicated.

> **"Great minds discuss ideas; average minds discuss events; small minds discuss people."**
>
> — *Eleanor Roosevelt*

Anna Eleanor Roosevelt (October 11, 1884 – November 7, 1962) was an American political figure, diplomat and activist. She served as the First Lady of the United States from March 4, 1933, to April 12, 1945, during her husband President Franklin D. Roosevelt's four terms in office, making her the longest-serving First Lady of the United States.

Roosevelt served as United States Delegate to the United Nations General Assembly from 1945 to 1952.

President Harry S. Truman later called her the "First Lady of the World" in tribute to her human rights achievements.

Roosevelt was a member of the prominent American Roosevelt and Livingston families and a niece of President Theodore Roosevelt. She had an unhappy childhood, having suffered the deaths of both parents and one of her brothers at a young age. At 15, she attended Allenwood Academy in London and was deeply influenced by its headmistress Marie Souvestre. Returning to the U.S., she married her fifth cousin once removed, Franklin D. Roosevelt, in 1905 and she became an influential figure to many, especially women.

"There is no better gift a society can give children than the opportunity to grow up safe and free-the chance to pursue whatever dreams they may have."

— *John Roberts*

John Glover Roberts Jr. (born January 27, 1955) is an American lawyer and jurist who serves as Chief Justice of the United States. Roberts has authored the majority opinion in several landmark cases. He has been described as having a conservative judicial philosophy but has shown a willingness to work with the Supreme Court's liberal bloc. Roberts presided over

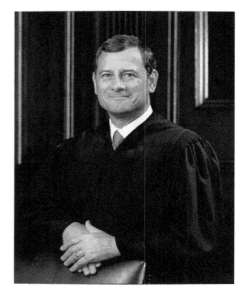

the impeachment trial of President Donald Trump.

Roberts grew up in northwestern Indiana and was educated in Catholic schools. He studied history at Harvard College and then attended Harvard Law School, where he was managing editor of the Harvard Law Review. He served as a law clerk for Circuit Judge Henry Friendly and then-associate justice William Rehnquist before taking a position in the attorney general's office during the Reagan Administration. He went on to serve the Reagan administration and the George H. W. Bush administration in the Department of Justice and the Office of the White House Counsel, before spending fourteen years in private law practice. He argued 39 cases before the Supreme Court during this time. Notably, he represented 19 states in United States v. Microsoft Corp.

"Sometimes in the past when I played something might make me lose focus, or I would go home after a game where I thought I could have played better and I would let it hang over my head for a long time when it shouldn't."

— *LeBron James*

LeBron Raymone James Sr. (born December 30, 1984) is an American professional basketball player for the Los Angeles Lakers of the National Basketball Association (NBA). He is widely considered to be one of the greatest basketball players in NBA history. Discussions ranking him as the greatest basketball player of all time have often been subject to significant debate, with frequent comparisons to Michael Jordan. James's teams have played in eight consecutive NBA Finals (2011–2018 seasons) and nine NBA Finals in total between the Miami Heat and Cleveland Cavaliers. His accomplishments include three NBA championships, four NBA Most Valuable Player (MVP) Awards, three Finals MVP Awards, and two Olympic gold medals. James holds the all-time record for playoffs points, is third in all-time points, and eighth in all-time assists. James was selected to the All-NBA First Team twelve times (all-time record), made the All-Defensive First Team five times, and has played in sixteen All-Star Games, in which he was selected All-Star MVP three times.

Biographical information Courtesy of Wikipedia, Britannica, and Brainy Quote

CHAPTER 4

Word Search, Crossword Puzzles, & Coloring

WORD SEARCH
Family and Friends

```
            A  u  N  T  s
         P  N  C  E  N  u  L  o
      R  D  E  s  I        s  M  o
   Z  F  V  H  R  T           H  s  B
S  s  E  L  C  N  u              C  T  J
R  K  N  Q  T  V  I              Q  C  N  V  C  W  s
R  E  M  V  B  R  O  T  H  E  R  s  Q  A  I  E  Q  K  H  I
E  H  Q  F  Z  u  Y  V  A  C  A  T  I  O  N  I  D  I  Q  V  E
R  H  T  T  C  V  L  u  Z  W  s  I  s  T  E  R  s  K  u  R  B  L
P  T  A  Q  C  R  G  R  A  N  D  M  O  T  H  E  R  W  u  T  C  R
Q  O  F  J  K  O  u  Z  T  J  G  R  A  N  D  D  A  D  D  Y  s  J
A  M  J  Q  E  C  D  H  E  Z  Z  D  s  N  I  s  u  O  C  G  K  u
V  A  K  T  T  L  N  C  N  W  s  Q  B  H  L  F  I     F  E  Z
M  M  Q  X                       C  A  I     O
   V  P                          s  T
```

BROTHERS	UNCLES	GRANDDADDY
SISTERS	AUNTS	VACATION
MOTHER	COUSINS	STUDENTS
FATHERS	GRANDMOTHER	

WORD SEARCH
Civil Rights

```
U  I  R  I  H  U  M  B  L  E  P  N  V  Z  F
H  T  F  B  G  C  W  U  H  L  H  M  N  C  Z
W  U  J  C  W  O  I  X  P  A  I  U  U  V  M
P  D  P  W  C  K  S  K  I  P  M  W  K  D  E
U  J  R  O  N  G  F  N  E  Q  C  I  I  W  M
O  I  D  S  A  L  R  H  H  C  Z  J  M  I  U
T  P  A  R  T  I  C  I  P  A  T  E  B  C  W
H  G  Y  R  S  J  D  B  P  L  E  H  N  K  S
E  X  V  G  A  H  I  L  B  V  M  T  L  F  H
R  J  G  Z  Y  D  N  B  E  S  Q  W  Z  M  Y
S  Z  Z  H  U  C  I  I  L  A  D  E  V  I  G
P  P  Y  U  G  V  H  A  G  L  Z  T  W  Q  B
E  T  A  E  R  C  O  P  T  Z  P  E  I  V
D  A  X  D  A  G  V  U  D  E  J  M  V  P  K
S  J  P  D  Q  A  O  N  A  H  Z  T  F  X  Z
```

HUMBLE	ACHIEVE
GIVE	GOALS
HELP	RADIATE
OTHERS	CREATE
PARTICIPATE	

Dr. Stephen L. Bond

WORD SEARCH
Civil Rights Activists 1

```
C P O S U P N W O Q J D Z V Y Y H B Z T H K K R I
P V V G S J S F M N X I D B U F F E U D W E N E T
I Q N K F A Z Y P Y V B T Q E C U N S U S G P H N
G I V U L U P Y V L H S A N D V Y J W L I M F T F
K E C E F R A N K L I N G Z O D W A T X C D R O P
T Z M L J E R O N T T Y B D T E K M Z F V O I R Q
W U P T N Y K T Z U K R I C A L V I G C I F F B Z
Q O M N G X S P I P E H P J G K Q N Y N M H L X V
X T J Y H T O R O D R M S N F J B J U H U R X L R
M L O C L A M A G R W J V H I M Q J Q T O X E H N
W H I K I U W H X S J X T J A T Q T N S N U V D N
C M Y D M W E S K G K A N N U J R T A W C X E P W
O D L Q C V C J U O F L K F D R O A C L X F Q K P
Y U R Z H R C O Z J C E A F E C A E M Q V B I N P
B C S S N E P O F J J O H N R E N A I D B Q T H G
H H O S V M W O D S K Q K L F M N L K T Q E H E P
L O P V P J Z N P L X K Q L L V N O H A F A L I T
C R A C F U R P L V J B S H A D I O W A A S E G H
N S A G M Q E E K T Y J S B R O G D S R I E W H F
S M X F Z R M N R A V A K R B C H V M Y V K I T P
T X C G H J R B E U G M V F X T H B F E A Z S M W
C P V O T W A G H B U E C W U O A A R P D V L Y L
F Z O G Z C F O T X I S Z T O R P S V M Y G H O G
C V N S I J U K U C E O S X O T G C A I B H A K Z
V Q K I F Y D H L C R C G H E I A U O S S J D R T
```

DOCTOR	LEWIS	PARKS	HEIGHT
MARTIN	BROTHER	MEDGAR	ALFRED
LUTHER	MALCOLM	EVERS	SHARPTON
KING	DIANE	JAMES	BENJAMIN
JUNIOR	NASH	FARMER	FRANKLIN
JOHN	ROSA	DOROTHY	CHAVIS

WORD SEARCH
Civil Rights Activists 2

```
M X W U O J O M C L K A T B Z W R D V X H J S N Q
Q S A D K S W K U W R N V A K B T C N R N F P N N
K S I G Y C Z D G V J T L M R A C Y D R A Z R A G
H H C D A W N H Y E A O M T U S Y E R O N I C D N
Q Q I P G B A Y U T B D G A R J Y K M W S M R E I
Y O L M T Z R W N A T J J H O L Q M A R H P H I T
J Y A K G Z M O P R X E N A Y G T N F T P H S R U
L L X J V S G A U G H K B M O O M D U R L H I F E
P X Y F A D N R N Q A H T I A K Y J C I A B E W O
U T W C R C I K D D M N A A T L B F E H R Q K Q G
I R E I A O K C F U E E E L A H T J A S M R S M H
D K W B S J T S F T R L M J B H Y D V F G G T E O
C N V I Z H V E O R H K A D B E K O F M Q S U F X
D K G A Q X T Y V N C A O A U N R G Y M F I L N P
Z E P S X S S N D J Z X R I Q B A N M Q G B E E W
Q N A O K L L A O H Z W O O A D O K A G T V O C B
S S N H W I X M Z E A S L D B J T I Y T C E B E K
A F B L D I Q B V M X R X W J E M B S L H F Z H R
E I N N A F A U G T P S R X R O D A J E J Y M S V
B K A J O P M T K J R T L I B B T G Z D L U R X N
O H V P F H T X E S Z E T N E T P X Z R M H I E V
G U J G I T N S C C H K K U E T T K Q W H O J V X
N O X N E L S O N Y A E C R A L V F O V N W G N L
B L J L X E T G G F B S O P A C P R R C R V T U G
S X L O G T X D V F S C V Y A P P M U P W W P K L
```

WEB DEBORAH FRIEDAN HARRIET
DUBOIS PARKER FANNIE TUBMAN
JESSE CORETTA LOU ALICIA
JACKSON SCOTT HAMER GARZA
MAHATMA KING NELSON RALPH
GANDHI BETTY MANDELA ALBERNATHY

WORD SEARCH
Living Life With True Happiness 1

```
W Z H H C X N X B S S P Y J K
Q G R D P O F K I N E C I K A
U R N P T V O N N E L L G I P
N I K I H A I I S N F Z I S L
K Q B E L F G J I J L Y U M F
W U C O C E O H D O E S Y I P
U D L A X M V F E Y S Q G L X
S T L I H L M A I H S V D E W
U T E V E X M O R A S P O J F
H D H W S B E A U T I F U L A
F V A X I Y E S S T W Y I V L
C R X B D L H F D E I F W C S
P O S H E Q D N Z V E W S N K
L X P V L Q O Z G C Q G X A H
C H A R M O N Y F G P G Y U M
```

TRAVELING	ENJOY
HARMONY	LIFE
BEAUTIFUL	SMILE
INSIDE	SELFLESS
OUT	KIND

WORD SEARCH
Society

N	E	E	L	L	S	C	H	O	L	A	R	L	Y
S	R	O	L	E	D	C	O	E	D	T	L	T	C
E	E	M	R	U	A	S	O	D	T	E	L	O	U
R	L	W	T	A	S	D	V	A	R	I	M	E	T
U	D	I	H	T	O	D	E	U	E	M	L	S	N
E	T	T	Y	T	E	O	T	R	E	H	N	L	E
D	T	C	I	V	T	A	D	N	S	O	O	T	M
O	A	S	O	E	R	O	T	D	R	H	O	T	E
R	A	T	A	E	A	E	W	L	D	R	I	N	T
A	E	M	T	P	D	T	N	R	S	E	T	P	A
D	E	I	R	O	T	I	W	O	D	C	O	R	T
S	L	T	L	R	V	M	E	W	D	L	A	E	S
U	N	I	T	E	D	S	T	A	T	E	S	T	A
N	U	V	O	R	E	S	U	E	A	E	E	V	R

LEADERSHIP   UNITED STATES

SCHOLARLY   STATEMENT

WORLD   DEVOTE

LITERATURE   COMMENTED

WORD SEARCH

Equality

M	E	Q	U	A	L	I	T	Y	C	O	C	D	C
Q	I	I	C	U	L	X	B	I	B	A	Y	I	O
X	L	E	G	I	S	L	A	T	I	V	E	S	M
A	L	M	C	M	T	U	A	R	N	C	C	C	M
E	A	S	Q	M	O	R	A	L	S	S	U	I	U
Y	I	E	N	M	C	L	S	L	A	S	R	P	N
I	A	I	C	A	C	T	I	V	I	S	M	L	I
B	E	E	S	L	L	L	M	M	Y	E	D	I	T
L	C	M	E	I	E	V	B	M	M	L	B	N	Y
C	E	X	P	R	E	S	S	I	O	N	P	A	M
B	I	O	S	T	S	Y	M	A	L	O	R	A	
N	O	M	S	N	I	S	E	S	E	E	E	Y	M
O	E	C	O	N	O	M	I	C	M	I	F	E	A
S	L	A	R	E	V	S	M	R	O	F	E	R	A

BLM	ECONOMIC
EXPRESSION	ACTIVISM
REFORMS	DISCIPLINARY
MORALS	COMMUNITY
LEGISLATIVE	EQUALITY

WORD SEARCH
Hashtag

S	G	P	C	T	E	Y	P	R	T	O	D	A	A
D	T	L	G	M	I	Y	O	S	I	V	I	N	U
O	T	A	G	D	I	T	L	E	Y	R	V	T	I
N	U	T	A	I	T	I	I	D	O	E	E	O	E
A	R	F	T	S	N	S	T	U	U	S	R	I	A
T	L	O	H	T	L	R	I	C	Y	S	S	S	V
I	D	R	S	S	D	E	C	A	E	E	I	E	N
O	I	M	A	S	E	V	I	T	R	A	F	I	S
N	C	S	H	D	S	I	A	I	G	O	Y	I	M
S	R	F	N	S	I	N	N	O	R	A	I	D	O
N	F	V	D	R	G	U	S	N	L	R	N	C	N
N	O	I	S	I	V	E	L	E	T	T	G	S	A
M	O	I	G	O	V	E	R	N	M	E	N	T	U
O	N	O	I	T	A	R	E	C	R	A	C	N	I

INCARCERATION	POLITICIANS
TELEVISION	EDUCATION
DIVERSIFYING	DONATIONS
PLATFORMS	HASHTAG
UNIVERSITY	GOVERNMENT

Dr. Stephen L. Bond

WORD SEARCH
Civil Rights

M	M	T	T	C	E	M	E	N	T	O	R	A	N
T	D	G	E	O	M	O	V	E	M	E	N	T	I
S	A	O	T	O	Y	O	M	Y	C	I	L	O	P
T	C	T	L	O	I	E	I	L	N	M	C	M	N
H	T	I	H	S	E	C	A	N	A	L	O	P	O
G	I	M	O	I	E	V	C	E	E	I	Y	I	N
I	V	E	I	E	H	O	I	M	I	V	N	N	V
R	I	O	M	H	I	T	C	H	A	T	E	C	I
L	S	R	T	M	S	S	L	M	E	D	I	A	O
I	T	T	M	T	T	R	P	A	I	O	N	N	L
V	S	I	T	Y	O	H	I	N	I	N	I	O	E
I	S	E	I	I	R	V	L	C	S	C	I	I	N
C	S	C	H	P	Y	I	I	T	M	I	O	E	C
T	D	G	S	V	A	I	E	I	N	C	O	S	E

TIME	NONVIOLENCE
MOVEMENT	MEDIA
POLICY	ACIVISTS
HISTORY	CIVIL RIGHTS
MENTOR	SOCIAL

FUN FACTS

1

Across

3. To offer help, or reinforce
4. Nothing or empty
7. Exciting, amazing or marvelous
8. All types of matter exist in our
10. Smallest unit of matter

Down

1. Something you do when you're happy
2. The act of defeating an opponent
5. Participant in a marathon
6. Feeling of deep affection
9. Person that sells homes

FUN FACTS
2

Across

2. A critical and deep thinker
4. Currency
8. The use of peaceful means
9. A fixed payment from work

Down

1. Taking charge in group activities
3. Being independent
5. Round red, yellow, or green fruit
6. Place of business
7. A domestic or tamed animal

FUN FACTS

3

Across

3. What we do at night
5. The G.O.A.T.
6. An extra layer of warmth
7. Friend, or buddy
9. Black panthers' battle phrase
10. Someone who informs the youth

Down

1. Always; at all times
2. Kobe Bryants' alter ego
4. Digital athlete
8. A place where people swim

Ahmaud Arbery

Tamir Rice

George Floyd

Christian Taylor

Breonna Taylor

Crossword Puzzles' Answers

Fun Facts 1

ACROSS

3. To offer help, or reinforce = **Fix**
4. Nothing or empty = **Zero**
7. Exciting, amazing, or marvelous = **Wonderful**
8. All types of matter exist in our = **Universe**
10. Smallest unit of matter = **Atom**

DOWN

1. Something you do when your happy = **Smile**
2. The act of defeating an opponent = **Victory**
5. Participant in a marathon = **Runner**
6. Feeling of deep affection = **Love**
9. Person that sells homes = **Realtor**

Fun Facts 2

ACROSS

2. A critical, and deep thinker = **Intellectual**
4. Currency = **Cash**
8. The use of peaceful means = **Nonviolence**
9. A fixed payment from work = **Salary**

DOWN

1. Taking charge in group activities = **Leadership**
3. Being independent = **Individualism**
5. Round red, yellow, and green fruit = **Apple**
6. Place of business = **Work**
7. A domestic or tamed animal = **Pet**

Fun Facts 3

ACROSS

3. What we do at night = **Sleep**
5. The G.O.A.T = **King James**
6. An extra layer of warmth = **Coat**
7. Friend, or buddy = **Fellow**
9. Black Panther catchphrase = **Wakanda Forever**
10. Someone who informs the youth = **Teacher**

DOWN

1. Always; at all times = **Ever**
2. Kobe Bryant's alter ego = **Black Mamba**
4. Digital athlete = **Gamer**
8. A place where people swim = **Beach**

CHAPTER 4

Personal Journal

**Write down your thoughts on how the
COVID-19 pandemic affected you.**

FACE SHIELD CE

FACE SHIELD
CE

EPILOGUE

Despite all of the uncertainty and turmoil going on in our country, I am still very optimistic about our future. Although these unconventional times have been a challenge for me as well, such as losing an uncle to COVID-19, along with having lost my twin sister and my dad (both not COVID-19 related), I feel passionate that the world will return to normal again. It has been, to say the least, a difficult time in my life. I hurt in so many ways just like my students expressed their hurts in this book. Releasing this book has been a help to me, as well as to them. Many of my students have told me that they long for the daily interactions we used to share. I do as well. I look forward to greeting my students daily and communicating with them face to face again. It's one of the many joys of being a teacher. The rapport that I establish with each student and watching them mature into productive citizens are two of the main reasons I chose the profession. As I read each journal, I was amazed at the courage and honesty they shared. Their resounding voices can be felt on each page of this book. The fact that these young people had to persevere through such a turbulent school year that ended so abruptly, shows the resolve they possess.

The sudden halt of the school year was new and strange territory for me as a teacher. When sports, proms, and all of the activities that students look forward to at the end of the year were canceled, I could empathize with them. They have inspired me so much. I hope that after you have read this book that you will feel the same way, too.

It's such a blessing to know that there is a generation of young people who are so resilient even during these difficult times. As we continue to move forward, I wait in great expectation to see what they will do later on in their lives. Many of the students in this book will begin college in the next few weeks. They have told me how excited they are about starting this new, exciting journey. Several are going to the military to serve our country. Others have already joined the workforce and are doing well. As a teacher, I feel that my students are already off to a great start, and the sky's the limit for each of them. I wish them all much success in their future endeavors.

To my young people, continue to persevere. You have already withstood a big storm in your life and have prevailed. Undergoing changes in our society, such as social distancing and your state quarantining everyone, which restricted you from gathering with friends and loved ones, is extremely stressful. However, you've endured the pain. You've dealt with the anguish of not having a prom and had to adapt from conventional graduation to having a "drive-in" graduation, wearing a protective mask. And, you've dealt with public facilities, such as restaurants and theatres, being closed, hampering your social life. If you can persevere through all of that, I am quite confident that you can persevere through any life obstacle you may face in the future. My students, please know that I care for you. I believe in you, and I am rooting for you!

Dr. Stephen L. Bond

NOTES

1. All quotes in this book fall under the Fair Use Act. All photos and drawings used in this book are under public domain, stock images, and/or belong to the author.

2. Source: Wikipedia, Britannica, and Brainy Quote
   Wikipedia's text content, in a nutshell, can be used under the terms of the Creative Commons Attribution Share-Alike license (CC-BY-SA); unless otherwise indicated, it can also be used under the terms of the GNU Free Documentation License.

ABOUT THE AUTHOR

Dr. Stephen Bond is a book author and speaker and has been a Social Studies teacher for over twenty years. Born in New York City, he moved to North Carolina six years ago, where he currently teaches at Wilson Preparatory Academy in Wilson, NC. Stephen has always had a great interest in history and has published works before on the Civil Rights Movement and inequalities in the classroom. His current work focuses on his high school scholars' lives after the coronavirus pandemic ended the school year in March 2020.

Thank You From the Publisher

Thank you for reading an Arrie Publishing Company book. We hope you enjoyed this book, and we encourage you to share your thoughts with us or write a review. This book is available in Paperback and e-Book and is available wherever books are sold or you can visit our website at www.arriepublishingcompany.com to view and purchase more of our books.

CPSIA information can be obtained
at www.ICGtesting.com
Printed in the USA
BVHW051042190621
609959BV00008B/994